SINGER'S CHOICE

PROFESSIONAL TRACKS FOR SERIOUS SINGERS

Sing The Songs of

COLE PORTER

2102

He was attracted to music by the time he started attending Yale with one of his first originals being a football song for the University. While he wrote his first show in 1916, Porter spent the 1920s in Europe and only wrote music on an occasional basis for the next decade. However after he had a hit in 1928 with "Let's Do It", he finally began to take his talents seriously. Returning to the United States, Porter soon became a household name, writing for numerous shows.

Among his hits were 1932's "Night And Day," 1934's "I Get A Kick Out Of You", and "Begin The Beguine" (written in 1934 and a major hit record for Artie Shaw in 1938). Due to Porter's charm, his witty lyrics, and the way he could say so much without actually saying what he was hinting at, Porter was able to write lyrics that, if they had been less subtle, would never have been accepted in the 1930s and 40s. For example, many listeners at the time probably did not realize that "Love For Sale" is about a prostitute advertising herself, that "I Get A Kick Out Of You" is about being passionately addicted to someone, and that "You Do Something To Me" is not as innocent as it seems. Other Cole Porter hits of his prime years included 'You're The Top", "My Heart Belongs To Daddy", "Anything Goes", "I've Got You Under My Skin", "In The Still Of The Night" and "You'd Be So Nice To Come Home To". "Ev'ry Time We Say Goodbye" is a touching ballad from the World War II. years that is still performed often these days. Completely out of character for Porter was his 1944 composition "Don't Fence Me In". Cole Porter alternated between writing for Broadway shows and movies throughout his life, finding it fairly easy to write for both. He suffered a major setback in 1937 when a riding accident in which a horse crushed his legs and made it impossible for him to walk again, but he refused to retire and did his best to overcome his handicap. Porter continued to humorously tackle topics in his lyrics that few others of the era would touch. His songs for the 1948 production of Kiss Me Kate included "Too Darn Hot" (leading one to ask "Too darn hot for what?") and "Always True To You In My Fashion", a breezy and philosophical look at adultery. In the 1950s Porter wrote for the shows Can Can (including "I Love Paris") and Silk Stockings. His last major success was his score for the Bing Crosby movie High Society which included "True Love" and "I Love You Samantha". Due to his bad health, Cole Porter retired in 1958, passing away six years later at the age of 73. He would be quite happy to know that his sophisticated songs are still being constantly played today by performers ranging from jazz musicians and rock stars to cabaret and Broadway singers.

Scott Yanow,
author of 11 books including Swing,
Jazz On Film and Jazz On Record 1917-76

Sing The Songs of

COLE PORTER

C O N T E N T S

ISBN 978-1-941566-01-5

Night and Day

Words and Music by
Cole Porter

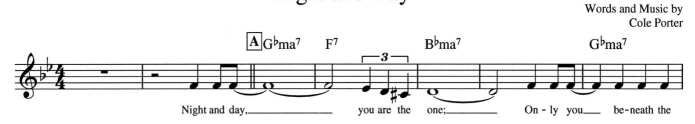

Night and day,_____ you are the one;____ On - ly you___ be-neath the

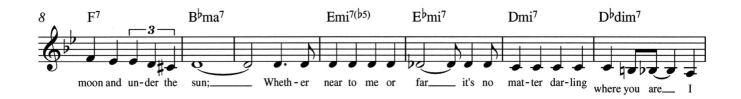

moon and un-der the sun;____ Wheth - er near to me or far____ it's no mat-ter dar-ling where you are___ I

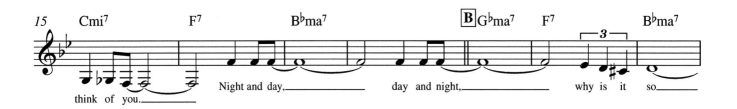

think of you. Night and day,_____ day and night,_____ why is it so____

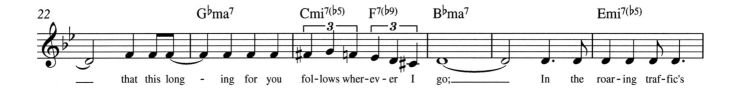

____ that this long - ing for you fol-lows wher-ev - er I go;_____ In the roar-ing traf-fic's

boom___ in the si-lence of my lone-ly room, I think of you. Night and day,_____ night and

day,_____ un-der the hide of me;____ There's an oh, such a hun-gry yearn - ing burn-ing in-

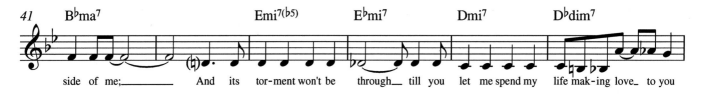

side of me;_____ And its tor-ment won't be through___ till you let me spend my life mak-ing love_ to you

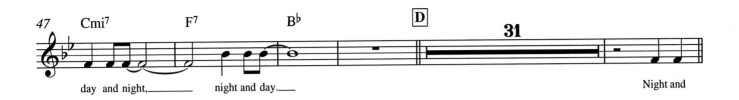

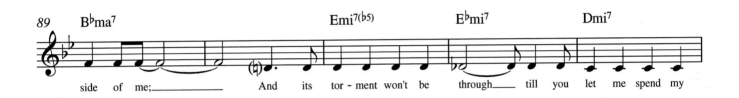

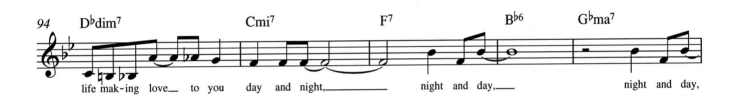

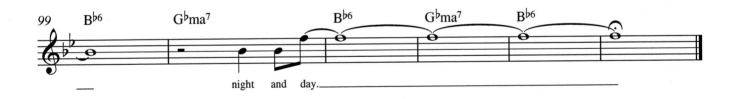

You Do Something To Me

Words and Music by
Cole Porter

You do some-thing to me; Some-thing that sim-ply mys-ti -

fies me; Tell me, why should it be you have the pow'r to hyp-no-tize

me. Let me live 'neath your spell; Do do___ that voo-doo___ that you do___ so

well; For you do some-thing to me that no-bod-y else can do.

Do do___ that voo-doo___ that you do___ so well; For

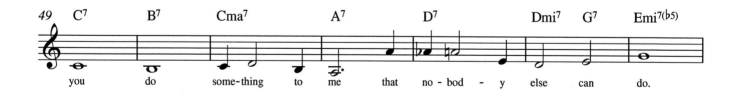

you do some-thing to me that no-bod-y else can do.

That no-bod-y else can do.

Just One Of Those Things

Words and Music by
Cole Porter

MMO 2102

8

Begin The Beguine

Words and Music by
Cole Porter

MMO 2102

10

MMO 2102

What Is This Thing Called Love?

Words and Music by
Cole Porter

MMO 2102

Let's Do It

Words and Music by
Cole Porter

13

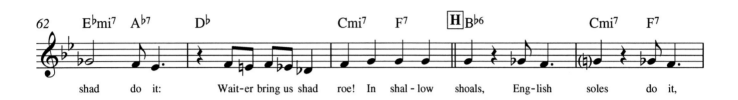

Love For Sale

Words and Music by
Cole Porter

I Get A Kick Out Of You

Words and Music by
Cole Porter

18

Other Great Songs from this MMO Series

Music Minus One
50 Executive Boulevard • Elmsford, New York 10523-1325
914-592-1188 • e-mail: info@musicminusone.com
www.musicminusone.com

MMO 2102   ISBN 978-1-941566-01-5